Framework Contract

This contract should be used for the appointment of one or more suppliers to carry out construction work or to provide design or advisory services on an 'as instructed' basis over a set term

An NEC document

April 2013

Construction Clients' Board endorsement of NEC3

The Construction Clients' Board recommends that public sector organisations use the NEC3 contracts when procuring construction. Standardising use of this comprehensive suite of contracts should help to deliver efficiencies across the public sector and promote behaviours in line with the principles of *Achieving Excellence in Construction.*

Cabinet Office UK

NEC is a division of Thomas Telford Ltd, which is a wholly owned subsidiary of the Institution of Civil Engineers (ICE), the owner and developer of the NEC.

The NEC is a family of standard contracts, each of which has these characteristics:

- Its use stimulates good management of the relationship between the two parties to the contract and, hence, of the work included in the contract.

- It can be used in a wide variety of commercial situations, for a wide variety of types of work and in any location.

- It is a clear and simple document – using language and a structure which are straightforward and easily understood.

NEC3 Framework Contract is one of the NEC family and is consistent with all other NEC3 documents. Also available are the Guidance Notes and Flow Charts.

ISBN (complete box set) 978 0 7277 5867 5
ISBN (this document) 978 0 7277 5901 6
ISBN (Framework Contract Guidance Notes and Flow Charts) 978 0 7277 5939 9

First edition June 2005
Reprinted 2007, 2010
Reprinted with amendments 2013

British Library Cataloguing in Publication Data for this publication is available from the British Library.

Typeset by Academic + Technical, Bristol

Printed and bound in Great Britain by Bell & Bain Limited, Glasgow, UK

CONTENTS

FOREWORD

I was delighted to be asked to write the Foreword for the NEC3 Contracts.

I have followed the outstanding rise and success of NEC contracts for a number of years now, in particular during my tenure as the 146th President of the Institution of Civil Engineers, 2010/11.

In my position as UK Government's Chief Construction Adviser, I am working with Government and industry to ensure Britain's construction sector is equipped with the knowledge, skills and best practice it needs in its transition to a low carbon economy. I am promoting innovation in the sector, including in particular the use of Building Information Modelling (BIM) in public sector construction procurement; and the synergy and fit with the collaborative nature of NEC contracts is obvious. The Government's construction strategy is a very significant investment and NEC contracts will play an important role in setting high standards of contract preparation, management and the desirable behaviour of our industry.

In the UK, we are faced with having to deliver a 15–20 per cent reduction in the cost to the public sector of construction during the lifetime of this Parliament. Shifting mind-set, attitude and behaviour into best practice NEC processes will go a considerable way to achieving this.

Of course, NEC contracts are used successfully around the world in both public and private sector projects; this trend seems set to continue at an increasing pace. NEC contracts are, according to my good friend and NEC's creator Dr Martin Barnes CBE, about better management of projects. This is quite achievable and I encourage you to understand NEC contracts to the best you can and exploit the potential this offers us all.

Peter Hansford

UK Government's Chief Construction Adviser
Cabinet Office

PREFACE

The NEC contracts are the only suite of standard contracts designed to facilitate and encourage good management of the projects on which they are used. The experience of using NEC contracts around the world is that they really make a difference. Previously, standard contracts were written mainly as legal documents best left in the desk drawer until costly and delaying problems had occurred and there were lengthy arguments about who was to blame.

The language of NEC contracts is clear and simple, and the procedures set out are all designed to stimulate good management. Foresighted collaboration between all the contributors to the project is the aim. The contracts set out how the interfaces between all the organisations involved will be managed – from the client through the designers and main contractors to all the many subcontractors and suppliers.

Versions of the NEC contract are specific to the work of professional service providers such as project managers and designers, to main contractors, to subcontractors and to suppliers. The wide range of situations covered by the contracts means that they do not need to be altered to suit any particular situation.

The NEC contracts are the first to deal specifically and effectively with management of the inevitable risks and uncertainties which are encountered to some extent on all projects. Management of the expected is easy, effective management of the unexpected draws fully on the collaborative approach inherent in the NEC contracts.

Most people working on projects using the NEC contracts for the first time are hugely impressed by the difference between the confrontational characteristics of traditional contracts and the teamwork engendered by the NEC. The NEC does not include specific provisions for dispute avoidance. They are not necessary. Collaborative management itself is designed to avoid disputes and it really works.

It is common for the final account for the work on a project to be settled at the time when the work is finished. The traditional long period of expensive professional work after completion to settle final payments just is not needed.

The NEC contracts are truly a massive change for the better for the industries in which they are used.

Dr Martin Barnes CBE

Originator of the NEC contracts

ACKNOWLEDGEMENTS

The first edition of the NEC Framework Contract was drafted by Peter Higgins working on behalf of the Institution of Civil Engineers, with the assistance of Les Eames and Dr Martin Barnes.

The original NEC was designed and drafted by Dr Martin Barnes then of Coopers and Lybrand with the assistance of Professor J. G. Perry then of The University of Birmingham, T. W. Weddell then of Travers Morgan Management, T. H. Nicholson, Consultant to the Institution of Civil Engineers, A. Norman then of the University of Manchester Institute of Science and Technology and P. A. Baird, then Corporate Contracts Consultant, Eskom, South Africa.

The Flow Charts were produced by Robert Gerrard with assistance from Ross Hayes and Tom Nicholson.

The members of the NEC Panel are:

P. Higgins, BSc, CEng, FICE, FCIArb (Chairman)
P. A. Baird, BSc, CEng, FICE, M(SA)ICE, MAPM
M. Barnes, BSc(Eng), PhD, FREng, FICE, FCIOB, CCMI, ACIArb, MBCS, FInstCES, FAPM
A. J. Bates, FRICS, MInstCES
A. J. M. Blackler, BA, LLB(Cantab), MCIArb
P. T. Cousins, BEng(Tech), DipArb, CEng, MICE, MCIArb, MCMI
L. T. Eames, BSc, FRICS, FCIOB
F. Forward, BA(Hons), DipArch, MSc(Const Law), RIBA, FCIArb
Professor J. G. Perry, MEng, PhD, CEng, FICE, MAPM
N. C. Shaw, FCIPS, CEng, MIMechE
T. W. Weddell, BSc, CEng, DIC, FICE, FIStructE, ACIArb

NEC Consultant:

R. A. Gerrard, BSc(Hons), MRICS, FCIArb, FCInstCES

Secretariat:

A. Cole, LLB, LLM, BL
J. M. Hawkins, BA(Hons), MSc
F. N. Vernon (Technical Adviser), BSc, CEng, MICE

AMENDMENTS APRIL 2013

The following amendments have been made to the June 2005 edition. Full details of all amendments are available on www.neccontract.com.

Page	Clause	Line	
1	20.1	1	replace paragraph
2	22	1	replace 'Package Order' with 'Quotation'
	22.1	1	replace clause
	22.2	1	replace clause
	22.3	1	replace clause
	22.4	1	delete clause
3	1st bullet point	2	replace 'June 2005' with 'April 2013'

CORE CLAUSES

Actions	**10**	
	10.1	The *Employer* and the *Supplier* shall act as stated in this contract and in a spirit of mutual trust and co-operation.

Identified and defined terms **11**

11.1   In these conditions of contract, terms identified in the Contract Data are in italics and defined terms have capital initials.

11.2   (1) The Parties are the *Employer* and the *Supplier*.

(2) Framework Information is information which specifies how the Parties work together and is in the document which the Contract Data states it is in.

(3) A Work Package is work which is to be carried out under this contract.

(4) A Package Order is an instruction to carry out a Work Package.

(5) A Time Charge Order is an instruction to provide advice on a proposed Work Package on a time charge basis.

Communications **13**

13.1   Each instruction, submission, notification, reply and other communication which this contract requires is communicated in a form which can be read, copied and recorded.

13.2   A communication has effect when it is received at the last address notified by the recipient for receiving communications or, if none is notified, at the address of the recipient stated in the Contract Data.

The Parties' obligations **20**

20.1   When the *Employer* requires work to be carried out within the *scope*, he provides the additional Contract Data specific to the work and selects a supplier using the *selection procedure*.

20.2   The *Supplier* obeys an instruction which is in accordance with this contract and is given to him by the *Employer*.

20.3   The *Supplier* attends meetings with the *Employer* and others as stated in the Framework Information.

Time Charge Order **21**

21.1   If he requires advice from the *Supplier* for a proposed Work Package, the *Employer* issues a Time Charge Order to the *Supplier*.

core clauses

contract data

Quotation 22

22.1 When instructed by the *Employer*, the *Supplier* submits a quotation in accordance with the *quotation procedure*. The *Supplier* submits details of his assessment with the quotation. The assessment is made using the *quotation information*. The *Employer* replies to the submission within one week of receiving the quotation. His reply is

- issue of a Package Order accepting the quotation,
- an instruction to submit a revised quotation or
- a notification that the proposed Package Order will not be issued to the *Supplier*.

22.2 If a quotation is to be revised, the *Employer* advises the *Supplier* of the reasons for not accepting the quotation and the *Supplier* submits a revised quotation within one week of receiving the *Employer's* reply.

22.3 The *Supplier* does not do any work included in a proposed Work Package until he has received a Package Order.

Completion 30

30.1 After the *end date*,

- the *Employer* may not issue a Time Charge Order or Package Order,
- the *Supplier* completes time charge work and Work Packages ordered before the *end date*.

Termination 90

90.1 Either Party may terminate their obligations under this contract at any time by notifying the other Party.

90.2 After a Party has notified termination,

- the *Employer* may not issue a Time Charge Order or Package Order and
- the *Supplier* completes time charge work and Work Packages ordered before the notification.

CONTRACT DATA

Part one – Data provided by the *Employer*

The Data which will apply to all work under the Framework Contract is

- The conditions of this contract are the clauses of the NEC3 Framework Contract April 2013.
- The *Employer* is

  Name ....

  Address ....

  ....

- The Framework Information is in...................................

  ....

- The *scope* is in...

  ....

- The *selection procedure* is in ....

  ....

- The *quotation procedure* is in ....

  ....

- The *end date* is ....

The Data which will apply to all Time Charge Orders is

(Include the Contract Data part one entries from the NEC Professional Services Contract for main Option E and the other Options selected.)

The Data which will apply to all Package Orders is

(Include the Contract Data part one entries for the Options selected from the NEC Contract to be used for a Works Package.)

nec®3 Framework Contract

Part two – Data provided by the *Supplier*

The Data which will apply to all work under the Framework Contract is

- The *Supplier* is...

  Name ....

  Address ....

- The *quotation information* is in ....

The Data which will apply to all Time Charge Orders is

(Include the Contract Data part two entries from the NEC Professional Services Contract for main Option E and the other Options selected.)

The Data which will apply to all Package Orders is

(Include the Contract Data part two entries for the Options selected from the NEC Contract to be used for a Works Package.)

core clauses

contract data

Part two – Data provided by the *Supplier*

⬤nec®3 Framework Contract

Index by clause numbers (main clause heads indicated by **bold** numbers). Terms in *italics* are identified in the Contract Data, and defined terms have capital initial letters.